MW01047240

CANADIAN WORKPLACE CULTURE
Mastering the Unspoken Rules

Matt Adolphe

BOLD WORLD BOOKS
RED DEER, ALBERTA

Published by:
Bold World Books
A division of Chinook Solutions Inc.
Red Deer, Alberta, Canada
www.boldworldbooks.com

Cataloguing in Publication Data
A catalog for this publication is available from the National Library of Canada

ISBN: 978-0-9868528-4-8

Manufactured in Canada

Printed on FSC certified paper

Printed and bound in Canada

Cover design by Chris Hobbs BFA

2 3 4 5 6 7 8 9 10

Table of Contents

Dedication

To my loving wife, Veronica, and our dear children, Joseph, Edward, and Gabriella.

Acknowledgements

This book is very much the product of a long journey, inspired by many people along the way. First and foremost, my deepest appreciation goes to my wife, Veronica who was incredibly helpful in the earlier editing of the manuscript. She is truly my best friend and inspiration for all things. Likewise, I want to thank our children, Joseph, Edward and Gabriella for being such an amazing part of our lives. Also, thanks to my parents and my brother Joe, who were as supportive throughout the process as they have been throughout my life.

I'm also grateful to Pamela Heath, SAIT's manager of English Language Foundations, who encouraged me to produce seminars and course material for her students, and motivated me to write this book. I am indebted to Roger Spielmann, my Professor of Indigenous Studies at Laurentian University. His course *An Introduction to Indigenous Studies* was my first course at University and his insights truly inspired my appreciation of cultural differences. I still remember the stories he shared about his own experiences. I think that is when my deep interest in culture really took flight.

I'd like to thank my editor, Caroline Kaiser, who did a remarkable job of making the ideas flow seamlessly. Special thanks to the brilliant publishing team at Bold World Books, Angela and Lawrence Hobbs. They are extremely insightful and generous, and I feel very fortunate to have been able to work with them. And finally I wish to thank every one of my students whom I have had the privilege of teaching. I have to say, they have all taught me far more than I could have ever taught them. Thank you all!

Matt Adolphe,

Calgary

June 2013

Introduction

Have you ever found yourself wondering why Canadians don't use car horns that often? Or why simple statements end with "eh"? Or why religion or politics are seldom discussed in depth? Or why many people cannot even bring themselves to watch leadership debates? Why do Canadians find themselves agreeing with their friends, family, and colleagues just to avoid a conflict? Why do they always seem to weigh whether an issue is worth fighting for? And why is the weather the most common topic of conversation? The answers to these questions define Canadian culture; knowing the answers helps you understand and be successful in it.

We can see the influence of Canadian culture everywhere. I remember when my son, Edward, was in kindergarten, and the teacher asked him to make a little presentation about what he wanted to be when he grew up. Edward thought about it and told us he wanted to be a chef. We thought that was great! However, when the day came to tell the class, he started to draw a picture of a firefighter.

His mother asked him what he was drawing:

"This is a picture of what I want to be when I grow up."

"But Edward, I thought you wanted to be a chef."

"Oh, that's our family secret, every boy in the class wants to be a firefighter; I just don't want to look different."

Those who come from cultures with more *direct* communication styles may be upset that my son hid his true desire to be a chef; but if you understand Canadian culture, you will know why he did.

I once had a foreign student who compared Canadians to peaches - soft on the surface, but a little hard in the middle. In her experience, Canadians seemed friendly to work with, but wanted little to do with her outside of work. Is this true? Do we like our colleagues but not want to be friends with them outside of work? If so, this may seem a bit odd to some people.

My student's experience shows that maintaining work relationships here takes as much hard work as the actual work people are hired to do. Building strong workplace relationships is hard work, critical to success and not to be taken lightly.

Canadian Workplace Culture: Mastering the Unspoken Rules explores the Canadian workplace in an effort to help you understand your work environment and find more success in it. Wherever you work, you'll find the culture varies depending on the presence of certain personalities and cultural groups. This book covers the topic broadly and identifies the unspoken rules that will help you achieve success within your workplace. To achieve that success, you must be willing to take an honest look at yourself and how you fit into the larger picture. It takes a great deal of courage to look inward and admit that you may need to change. In the end, a culture doesn't adapt to you, you need to adapt to it.

If you don't quite "fit" into your Canadian workplace, reading this book will help you see yourself a little more clearly, better understand how you are perceived by those around you, and know how to "fit in" a little better. The fact is to succeed in the workplace here you really need to weigh your words carefully, read between the lines, and be mindful of non-verbal cues. Ignoring any of these creates problems for you and others, but that's just the nature of our Canadian culture.

I invite you to read on and see what you can take from this material. Perhaps, like my students, you can take two or three points and start applying them immediately. There is a lot of information, and some of it may be new to you. If so, really try to think about how you can start to stretch yourself a little more. For those readers who feel they already understand these ten rules, I'm happy to hear that. You're probably pretty successful in your careers. However, please use this material to help others achieve that same level of success. After all, we are all in this together, and helping everyone to see that makes a culture even stronger.

Rule 1:
Put the Feelings of Others First

Canada has an empathetic culture, and people really live by the golden rule, "Do unto others as you would have them do unto you." With this in mind, get into the habit of asking and answering questions in your head: "How would this person like to receive this information?" or "Is this issue important enough to warrant disagreement?" or "What would I gain from correcting her?" or "Is it important to express my opinion, or should I just go along with hers?" Yes, this is how you need to think about conversations in the Canadian workplace.

The most successful business managers and supervisors have these questions in mind when they talk to colleagues, subordinates, and especially superiors. On the other hand, people who just speak their minds are probably having issues with their colleagues, whether they know it or not.

Putting other people first in your discussions isn't always easy. The process is complicated by those who just keep talking. They miss the fact that you are putting them first out of politeness, not necessarily out of real interest in what they have to say. Some may even take advantage and dominate the conversation when you put them first. What should you do?

You still want to put people first. Here's an example of how to do it. Imagine that you just had a great weekend and want to share the details. You come to work and see a colleague who usually enjoys hearing about your life. However, today this colleague looks a little unhappy, and when she says, without much enthusiasm:

"How was your weekend?"

This is when you should forget about your weekend and say:

"My weekend wasn't bad – how about yours? Is everything okay?"

The idea here is to put others first at all times. Read their non-verbal clues and be prepared to put your interests aside.

What kind of non-verbal signs should you look for? Just learn to notice the overall appearance and tone of voice of the other person. If she looks a bit tired, her shoulders are drawn down, or there is an unusual hesitancy in her voice, perhaps her weekend wasn't as good as yours. In this case, you may want to put the subject of your fascinating weekend aside and just allow yourself to be a listener. Don't probe and don't make observations about her appearance and tone of voice – just listen to what she has to say.

Give her your utmost attention. If you really have to go, indicate that it was nice having a talk together and that you would like to continue the conversation at another time. Finish by offering some words of encouragement, for example, "Hey, have a great morning, and let's catch up later." Even if she really didn't say much at all, your effort to put her first will leave her with a pleasant feeling about you and maybe even a little smile. Leaving someone with a smile, or a comment that shows you were listening, makes you the kind of friendly and empathetic person that Canada is known for.

You often hear that Canadians are so polite and friendly, but what is it that leads people to believe this? True empathy and concern for putting the feelings of others first fosters this image. Even if we cannot really define Canadian culture, empathy and concern are the very foundation of it. By understanding that and contributing to it, you will be successful in your life here, and everyone will gain from your sense of compassion for others. In fact, understanding how Canadians communicate empathetically is a major advantage in succeeding in the Canadian workplace.

Another aspect of putting people first is being mindful of whether you *ask* or *tell* someone to do something. Get in the habit of asking, not telling. If you want someone to do something, ask them if they wouldn't mind doing it, instead of telling them to do it. Don't worry; in a culture where people communicate indirectly, asking is how we instruct people to do things.

If you are from a culture in which people communicate or do things in a direct way, you might be afraid that if you ask someone to do something, they'll say no. But Canadians, as well as people from other cultures with indirect communication styles, realize that even though you are asking them to do something, they are actually being *told* to do something. For example, a supervisor might ask:

"Would you mind working a few more hours tonight?"

This means you need to, so you would respond as if you were told to do it and say:

"Sure, no problem!"

Asking people to do things rather than telling them is a common courtesy both in the workplace and outside it.

The point here is, in a conflict-averse culture (one, like Canada's, where conflict is actively avoided), you have to do whatever you can to make other people feel at ease. Always be aware that people truly want to be treated the same way they treat others, so make every effort to do so. If someone gives you a compliment, remember it and return the favour when you can – just make sure you don't look as if you are expecting something in return.

This may be difficult for newcomers or those not used to this less direct way of dealing with people. How do you find the balance between being considerate to others while simultaneously being indirect and possibly appearing sincere? Understanding this question and being able to find this balance is a clear sign that you are a decent communicator, and you actually do care more about others than you do about yourself.

Conversations in the workplace are true opportunities to show that you are always willing to put others first. We have all had those conversations with people who always try to present a more exciting or interesting story than ours. When you mention your holiday, theirs is always more exotic. This sort of competition is tragic because these people have no idea that others are actually having a hard time talking to them. These are the same individuals who may say things in meetings just to sound important. They believe people like to hear their opinions. And because they feel more important than others, they miss all the clues people are giving them.

For example, once I was teaching a class on Canadian culture when Robert, a bright Canadian born student, asked:

"I've been working at my current job for several years, and my manager always told me that I'd make a great supervisor, yet I've never been promoted. Why is that?"

"Well Robert, you seem to be very hard working and outgoing, I'll need to give your question some thought."

A few weeks later I found my answer when I overheard his conversation with his shy classmate, Joe:

"I think the best hamburgers in town are at Burger Bob's!"

"What? Those burgers are terrible, Joe!"

Joe lowered his head, looked at the ground and sadly, dejectedly replied:

"Well... I like them."

Robert probably wasn't getting promoted because he wasn't going along with workplace expectations. Many of his conversations were probably just like this one, making him appear aggressive. Without realizing it he himself pushed promotions out of his reach and created his workplace struggle.

It isn't hard to put others first, just take the time to ask yourself a few questions:

1. How would I wish to be treated if the roles were reversed?
2. Do I see the value in being concerned about other people's feelings?
3. How much extra time does it take to be a little less direct and more mindful of others' feelings?
4. How do I want to be perceived by my colleagues?
5. How much will I gain by being direct and possibly upsetting the other person?
6. How hard is it to use a few new strategies from this book to communicate with my colleagues?
7. Is considering the emotions and well-being of others really an inconvenience?
8. Do I only care about myself? If your answer is no, then perhaps you should improve the way you communicate – put the feelings of others first.

When communicating, always consider the result you want to achieve. We all want to succeed in our relationships, and with every relationship come some sacrifices. In Canada, if you have a habit of putting people first and being a good listener, you become a valuable part of any team and a natural leader in the eyes of the people you work for.

Self-reflection – Do You Put Others First?

So here you are. You now know how people communicate in Canada. The next step is using that knowledge to avoid conflict. You put the feelings of others first because it creates an environment of trust and thoughtfulness. And within that environment, people can cope well with one another. When you fail to put the feelings of others first, you appear self-centred and not a team player. This creates stress for those around you. Therefore, before you move on to learning how to avoid conflict, ask yourself these questions:

1. Do you think it is important to make the people around you feel comfortable?
2. Do you have compassion and empathy for others – even strangers?
3. Do you want to be regarded as caring, understanding, and sympathetic?
4. Are you accepting of personality differences?

Or

1. Do you take pleasure in correcting others – even on small matters?
2. Do you routinely believe that you are the smartest person in the room?
3. Do you feel you have a duty to be completely straightforward at all times, and that anything less is dishonest?
4. Is your ideal world a place where everyone speaks directly about whatever is on their mind, no matter how hurtful?

If you answered yes to the first four questions, you are more apt to avoid conflict than not. However, if you answered yes to the last four questions, avoiding conflict is clearly not your priority. This should be a concern for you because you are living and working in a culture in which people avoid conflict. Actually, you are living in a culture that rewards, and even promotes, those who successfully *avoid* conflict. Let's consider this subject in Rule 2.

Rule 2:
Understand Indirect Communication

On the whole, Canadians try to be indirect when they communicate to avoid hurt feelings and possible conflict. In fact, Canadians tend to avoid topics that can even lead to conflict. Because of this, Canadians appear to those from other cultures as unconcerned with issues. But it is very hard to judge a culture when you are on the outside looking in; you need to be living and working in a place to fully understand how a culture operates.

Canadians express negative emotions through hints or non-verbal communication, rather than by just saying no or "I disagree." They may hem and haw or shift uncomfortably in their chairs. True Canadians even avoid the word "but" when giving negative feedback, either in person or in emails. For example, instead of saying, "I see what you are trying to say, *but* I think..." they might say, "I see what you are trying to say. What I am thinking is..." In other words, just don't use "but", start a new sentence instead. Canadians don't like the word *but* because it erases the positive statement you just started your feedback with. Try to omit the word *but* when you are disagreeing or giving negative feedback.

Also, a true friend in Canada goes to great lengths to make his friend feel good about himself. For example, when I am feeling heavier than usual, I might ask my friend, "Do I look fat?"

My friend will dutifully reply, "Come on! You look fine! What are you talking about?" Yes, even among close friends, focusing on the positive is an important feature of interpersonal relationships.

Canadians reading this may think that focusing on the positive, by way of telling a white lie to spare another person's feelings, is the norm everywhere. However, in some cultures, people believe that telling someone he is fat helps motivate him to lose weight. That is why many immigrant children don't want to visit their parents' countries. They know that waiting for them at the airport will be an aunt who doesn't mind saying, "You look fat!"

In some cultures, avoiding conflict is seen as actual dishonesty and not the behaviour of a true friend at all. They believe that a true friend must be completely honest and forthright. Well, does this mean that Canadians are dishonest? *Not exactly.* For example, if you ask me for a reference letter and I shift my body and say, "Well, I can give you one if you can't get anyone else to," that means no. To communicate successfully, you must have the ability to pick up on inferences and non-verbal cues.

In cultures with indirect communication styles, yes sometimes means no. You can determine when this is the case by observing non-verbal cues. Watch how a person shifts in her chair or breaks eye contact, or even changes her tone of voice. A flat, indifferent voice most likely means no. Newcomers, or even Canadians brought up in households with direct communication as the norm, have issues with such lack of directness. They simply cannot understand why, if a person doesn't want to do something, she won't just say no.

Actually, the truth about what someone really means is in the eyebrows, other non-verbal cues, and what the person actually says. Let's go back to the example of the reference letter request. When you ask someone to provide a reference letter for you, and you are unsure if he wants to do it, just look at his eyebrows and listen to what he says and how he says it.

If his eyebrows raise only a little when he says, "Yeah, I suppose I can write you a reference," the eyebrows are considered neutral, and he means no. Pay attention to the word *suppose* too, it also tends to mean no.

On the other hand, if his eyebrows are raised, his voice changes to a higher pitch and he answers, "Absolutely! Do you have the name of the person you want me to address the letter to? Or do you just need my contact information?" he wants to write a letter for you. The pitch is higher, the tone is more enthusiastic, the eyebrows are raised, and eye contact is steadily maintained. This is a person you want to use as a reference. He has confidence in you and will say nice things about you.

The person in the first example is actually saying, "I really don't want to... *please pick up on that*." And if the company you are applying to work for were to actually phone him, his voice on the phone would likely give away his true opinion of you. A clever human resource person would pick up that this person isn't totally confident in your abilities.

So why wouldn't that person just say no? Canadians don't like conflict, so they would much rather not have negative conversations that may lead to conflict, especially at work. In short, read between the lines and expect less directness.

What isn't being said is the key to understanding how Canadians think, so be open to receiving messages in indirect ways. Negative feedback may come in the form of a hint. For example, "Boy, you have a strong handshake!" really means your handshake is too aggressive. "That's a really bright scarf!" means it is too out of step with fashion.

This indirect way of communicating can seem dishonest. The lack of straightforwardness can be very frustrating. However, Canadians communicate indirectly, so look beyond their words for information. Look at the non-verbal cues, especially the eyes. If someone looks down or away when answering you, they mean something other than what they are saying. Study these cues and become more observant. The truth may not be spoken! Understanding how people express a negative response in non-verbal ways helps you to succeed.

You'll notice that Canadians use a lot of facial expressions to fill in the gaps in a conversation. For example, if people are happy, it shows; if they are concerned, it shows; if they are slightly uncomfortable, it shows; if they feel you are being too direct and forceful with your ideas, it shows. Take time to observe facial expressions and try to find the other person's true feelings in them. For example, if someone is busy and needs to go, he may start looking over your shoulder. Try to observe those things. Facial expressions often give the best indication of a person's true feelings; however there are cultures where people don't use a lot of facial expressions.

In some Asian cultures, for example, showing anything but a neutral expression is rude. So how do these people adapt when they move to Canada? They need to make a conscious effort to adapt and understand that facial expressions are an important part of our communication. Canadians too need to do their part in being a little more patient and understanding because newcomers are moving here every day.

Adapting to a workplace is difficult, even for those born in Canada. To really build strong relationships here, you need to communicate on a variety of levels. In some cultures, people are very direct and tell you exactly what is on their minds, so the non-verbal cues are less important. Perhaps more than other cultures, Canadians communicate with vocal tones, pitch, non-verbal cues, and inferences to avoid negativity that could possibly lead to conflict.

If you are unsure if the words coming out of a person's mouth are truthful, scan the face. The answer is there. And if you don't use a lot of facial expressions, realize that sometimes people will initially be uncomfortable dealing with you. However, don't worry; people will warm up to you eventually and respect that you are different. Just realize that if your expression tends to be neutral, your first impression on Canadians may not be as positive as you would hope.

When you ask people to define Canadian culture, they use words like *friendly* and *polite*. However, let's look at the negative aspect of being this way. Maintaining that friendly and polite culture isn't easy; it relies on sacrifice, on everyone doing their bit to fit in and avoid conflict.

For people who like to be recognized for being direct and individualistic, fitting in can be hard to accept. They may think that they should be able to say and do whatever they please. But, if they don't make the effort to fit in, they may experience times when others feel uncomfortable dealing with them. Keep in mind that Canadians try to avoid conflict by showing each other how similar they are.

If you like to stand out and be recognized for being different, you may appear unaware of the cultural rules. Your very style sends a message that you are not that concerned about avoiding conflict, and others may start to avoid you. Colleagues may even distance themselves from you fearing that if they are close to you, others may think they are same as you. In the end, displaying an individualistic style creates stress for those around you – something that goes against the first rule: *Put the feelings of others first.*

Self-reflection – Are You Too Direct?

Take a deep breath and consider your life up to this point. Think about the connection between avoiding conflict and being a successful conversationalist, both in terms of giving and receiving information.

If you have lived your whole life in Canada, look back and remember an incident when someone was trying to tell you things indirectly, but you missed the message. Now, honestly ask yourself these questions:

1. What prevented me from getting the message?
2. Whose fault was it that I didn't get the message?
3. What was that person trying to tell me?
4. How might things be different in my life today if I had immediately understood the message?

If you are a newcomer or a Canadian raised in a more direct household trying to understand the concept of conflict avoidance, ask yourself the following questions:

1. Do I feel comfortable when people make an effort to avoid the negative and focus on the positive?
2. Am I open to receiving messages that may be indirect?
3. Do I see this indirect way of communicating as a form of politeness?
4. What am I doing to adapt to this style of communication in my conversations?

Take what you have learned so far and start thinking of ways to apply it in everyday conversations you have with colleagues. Let's talk strategy.

Rule 3:
Use Everyday Conversation Strategies

Ah, the weather – a Canadian's favourite topic of conversation! It is unlikely to lead to a hot debate, as it is neutral and safe. If you want to discover if someone understands the culture or the usual way Canadians communicate, discuss the weather. Bringing up this topic is a test to see if you are an agreeable person who knows the rules. It goes like this: I say, "It's a little hot today, eh?" There's only one answer in this scenario.

Think about it. It's the weather, the most mundane topic in the world. I have clearly expressed an opinion and asked for your agreement. Whether you think it's hot or not, the correct response is, "Yeah, it sure is." If you happen to decide that since you lived in a place that routinely gets to 25 degrees Celsius, which is actually considered a cold day there, you might say, "Actually, it doesn't seem that hot to me." In doing so, you might offend the other person.

Someone meeting you for the first time would think you are direct, reckless, not empathetic, or perhaps not from Canada. If you are from here, this might make you look especially bad, as people might not understand how you could be born and raised here, and not know enough to just say, "Yeah, it sure is."

Regardless of what happens next, you might have just hurt your relationship with that person. Depending on the type of person he is or the context, you could have created a very poor first impression. First impressions are really everything in Canada, and in most cases, your first impression is your lasting impression. Developing strong conversation skills really helps you make a positive impression.

This brings us to the topic of small talk, which globally isn't as common as Canadians might think. For many cultures around the world, there is actually no such thing as small talk; either you get down to serious business or you have a really heartfelt conversation.

Canadians born and raised here without much exposure to other cultures may have a hard time understanding that small talk is actually the default conversational mode of a culture with an indirect communication style. In Canada, small talk is used as a warm-up to a business meeting or as a mode of polite conversation among colleagues. In both cases, the topics are basic, generic, and without depth. They range from weather to movies and TV to some current events.

Using small talk in Canada is important because it shows others that you are non-confrontational and modest. During small talk, even about the simplest of topics, you should show interest and enthusiasm for the conversation. You may have an academic and professional background, but keep your conversation simple and light using vocabulary that doesn't make people reach for a dictionary. Some people, even those born in Canada, might find these types of conversations fake and a waste of time, but they miss the point. Small talk reveals you as non-threatening and down-to-earth. In Canada these characteristics are prized and admired.

Many people don't mind a little pleasant small talk, yet they are totally unaware of how important it is to be prepared for it. They may even think that the weather is the only thing they need to be ready to talk about. But although small talk tends to be about insignificant topics, they are topics you should be knowledgeable about. If you are not prepared to participate in small talk, you risk being out of touch with your colleagues.

So, if you work with people who follow the local hockey team, then keep up-to-date with that team's standings. If your colleagues chat about movies or particular actors, then watch those movies and know something about those actors. If you are not prepared for these conversations, or don't show an interest in small talk, you risk a great deal in your professional career. In fact, the way you make small talk before a job interview could even be the deciding factor in determining if you are fit for that particular company. In the Canadian workplace, being inept at small talk is seen as an unfortunate weakness.

Canadians often use even the most basic of everyday conversations to see if there is any hint that the other person is unaware of the rules. If you are deemed a failure at these types of conversations, you might be instantly judged and avoided.

What are the rules, you might ask? Well, try to be good at small talk by being sincerely engaged and active in the dialogue. For example, nod while others are talking, show enthusiasm for their points of view, and never interrupt them while they are speaking. These conversations should never feel forced or insincere either.

Small talk should move back and forth between people with both of them talking for equal amounts of time. Exchanges should be relatively short and lively. Don't be the person who doesn't listen enough, talking more than the other person to keep the focus on you and how much more interesting you are. Don't make it seem that you prefer the sound of your own voice to anyone else's. Also, try not to use yourself as an example when giving suggestions. Say, "Have you thought about trying to..." instead of, "Well, what I do is this..."

There are several other things you should avoid in conversations too. First, some people like to use foul language around everyone, but they need to buffer their language, especially around older people, superiors, and others who don't use foul language.

Second, some people, bored with everyday small talk, try to make things interesting by starting debates during breaks. Remember that people tend to like more polite and easygoing discussions during their breaks. So, steer clear of these *real issue* discussions – they're seldom worthy of debate. Occasionally, you do need to stand up for yourself and make a point; but most conversations should be pleasant and agreeable.

Third, some people like to organize after-work functions hoping for deeper conversations. Interestingly enough, they may be disappointed to discover these conversations – at a pub, let's say – look and sound much as they do in the lunchroom. In some cultures in which direct communication prevails, after work is a time to have deeper conversations that touch on issues you would not normally talk about in the office. But, for the sake of avoiding conflict, Canadians try to keep conversations light.

Fourth, some people make a point of disliking political correctness. But as language changes, groups of people want to be referred to in a different way; they want a new label. Someone who refuses to use that label looks stubborn, and sometimes even a little prejudiced.

Fifth, some people like to give unsolicited advice, and no one really likes that.

Sixth, some people talk *at* you rather than *with* you. It almost feels like your job is to listen and not contribute to the topic, as if your input is neither required nor appreciated.

And last, but not least, avoid conflict. Conversations in the workplace are opportunities to display humility, not individuality. Canadians prefer agreeable conversations where opinions are carefully worded. For example, if Jeremy sees a movie that doesn't interest Cathy, their conversation may sound like this:

"Hey, did you see the movie Vacation Time?"

Before answering, Cathy needs to look for clues in Jeremy's body language. If he obviously likes the movie, she'll say:

"Yeah, I did see it. It was pretty good... how did you like it?"

Notice the hesitation – that slight drop in enthusiasm tells Jeremy that Cathy did not like the movie. In turn, he should think about a new topic or movie to discuss:

"Yeah, I thought it was really good. So what did you do on the weekend?"

As you can see, a conflict has been avoided, nothing direct was said, and no one was hurt. That is how a typical Canadian workplace conversation takes place.

When Cathy said, "It was pretty good," but really did not think so, is that considered a lie? Someone from a more assertive culture might say, "Yes, absolutely, if Cathy did not like the movie she should just say so."

In Canada, Cathy clearly shows disinterest and Jeremy notices it, so both sides clearly understand one another without entering into conflict. That is considered a successful conversation, and neither Jeremy nor Cathy thinks of the other person as a liar.

Now, what happens if Cathy actually admits how much she disliked the movie? Here's what might happen:

"Hey, did you see the movie Vacation Time?"

"Yeah, I didn't like it very much; it was a little long and boring."

"Well... I liked it."

What does Cathy gain by making this an issue worth debating? Jeremy is clearly uncomfortable and might even start avoiding her completely. Because Cathy decides to give her opinion on such a trivial issue, it becomes clear to him that she cannot be trusted to be agreeable in any conversation. And now Cathy starts to notice that her relationship with Jeremy has changed and she doesn't understand what happened. The message here is to be as agreeable as you can. Nothing is really worth debating, especially if it makes the other person feel bad.

When we talk about the importance of being agreeable in conversations, this ultimately brings us to the real Canadian treasure: the sentence tag "eh?" Americans often find it amusing. However, they have their own tag in the form of "huh?" and the British have theirs as well, "isn't it?" Basically, these tags all have one thing in common: they are asking for confirmation. But the American and British ones don't have the deep cultural significance of the Canadian "eh?" which takes this asking to a very different level.

If a Canadian were to say, "That's a great pizza place, eh?" she is actually saying:

"I'm really putting myself out there by having a bold opinion about a particular subject. And in doing so, I'm leaving myself open for possible disagreement. So I would really appreciate it if you would just see that this is all over something simple, and I happen to just really like the place. So can you just do me the favour of agreeing with me, even though you may not actually feel the same way?"

In a culture in which people are more direct, if someone really didn't like that pizza place, he would tell you straight, regardless of the "eh?" It would be considered a lie to say otherwise. But being so forthright is a mistake with Canadians. If you really do want to disagree, recall the previous example with Cathy and Jeremy and say, "Yeah... it's pretty good... I've been there before." Now, the message has been sent, but was it even worth doing? Couldn't you simply have said, "Yeah! It is pretty good!" After all, who cares? It's just a pizza place. In Canada, you'll look like a good sport for letting others have their opinions. However, in cultures with a direct communication style, you might appear to be a pushover. Nevertheless, when in Rome, do as the Romans do.

Canadians sometimes show their displeasure by not returning simple everyday courtesies. For example, when you say hello to Pat every day and add, "How are you?" and Pat replies, "Good. And you?" that's a sure sign things are good between you and Pat. However, if you say to Pat, "How are you?" and Pat says, "Fine," there may be something wrong. Why doesn't Pat return the courtesy as always?

The answer is one of two things: Pat is just in a hurry or thinking about something else, or she may feel slighted by something you said or did and this is her way of telling you. Think about what Pat is communicating by configuring your brain to receive all kinds of indirect messages. If you only listen for straight answers and ignore subliminal ones, you put yourself at a serious disadvantage. And most importantly, when someone asks, "How are you?" always reply with, "Good. And you?" so that the other person doesn't wonder about your state of mind.

The rules are simple – make an effort to fit in and go with the flow. Learning everyday conversation strategies can really help you be more successful in your workplace relationships. These strategies are a universal necessity. No matter what culture you are living in, you need to adapt to the prevailing way of conversing. Wouldn't it be madness to do otherwise?

I suppose that some people may feel that since Canada is multicultural, there isn't one true Canadian culture. Yes, Canada is wonderfully diverse, but we have a culture of conflict avoidance here that children born or raised here from an early age instinctively realize. And although there are people of many different ethnicities living here, the Canadian workplace, like any workplace in the world, has deep-rooted rules that have been well established by previous generations and complex cultural influences. And there is reason to believe that regardless of the influx of immigrants, the Canadian way of communicating in the workplace will remain the status quo for years to come.

But why are some people who were born in Canada not able to grasp the rules? Perhaps they came from households where expressing themselves directly was the cultural norm, or they were told by their teachers that their sense of individuality was inspiring. I am not saying that individuality is uninspiring, nor am I saying that an assertive style of communicating is wrong; I'm just saying that being yourself in Canada requires a more cautious and modest approach. The key to success in any given work environment lies in understanding its parameters and working within them.

Self-reflection – What's Your Style?

Let's try to understand how everyday conversation strategies can help you fit into the workplace.

Take a moment to reflect on your conversational style:

1. During everyday conversation, do you feel it's important to be the best listener you can be?
2. Do you see everyday conversations as opportunities to show other people that you are interested in them?
3. Do you make small talk and sound humble and down-to-earth in your interactions with people?
4. Do you try to agree with others and avoid debates?

On the other hand:

1. Is it important for you to dominate a conversation by talking too much?
2. Do you use conversations as opportunities to show how interesting you are?
3. Do you like to insert odd expressions into conversations or use concepts that others may not understand?
4. Do you use foul language or show disdain for politically correct language?

If you find that you answered no to the first four questions and yes to last four, there is a good chance that you are not fitting into the workplace and may stand out as different or difficult to those around you.

However, if you answer yes to the first four questions and no to the last four, you are probably perceived as an empathetic and respectful individual.

Rule 4:
Don't Be Perceived as Arrogant

In the Canadian workplace, being referred to as arrogant happens for a variety of reasons. If you are perceived as arrogant you stand out, don't conform to accepted norms, and fail to go with the flow. In other words, you display your uniqueness in thinking, dressing, and communicating. It is far easier to do your own thing without considering the consequences, than it is to put yourself second to others. In the Canadian workplace, *arrogance* means showing a lack of respect for the status quo. The following examples highlight behaviours that might cause others to perceive you as arrogant:

1. You are always in high spirits, very playful, energetic, and laughing out loud. This is usually perceived by others as not working very hard – Canadians tend to be more emotionally neutral in the workplace.
2. You like to talk about yourself, your life, and your family. The less you focus on yourself and your family, the more likely it is you'll be perceived as a good listener.

3. Your clothes are a little different from those of everyone else you work with. Think of your colleagues' dress code as a team uniform. If you dress like them, you send the message that you are a team player.

4. You like people to know that you have special tastes; for example, you talk about a particular art form, type of food, or genre of film that is unfamiliar to most of your colleagues. When you do this, people may think you are trying to look smarter than they are.

5. You don't make an effort to remember people's names. Using names when talking to, or about others, is extremely important.

6. You complain a little too much. Some people in some cultures complain to show others how hard they work, but here complaining isn't the norm. Be flexible and work with conditions as they are, *or move on*.

7. You ask for help for things that you could probably do on your own. You will be perceived as lazy if you ask colleagues to do what you could figure out on your own.

8. You think you are irreplaceable, have an exaggerated sense of entitlement, and expect certain perks. If you let people know that you think you are the best at what you do, they may start to resent you.

9. You don't volunteer to help out at work functions. Be willing to sacrifice time to do small things for your company – in a cheerful way, and not because you think you have to.

10. When you start a new job, you question everything being done at that company, and you suggest changes. Later, when you have proven your loyalty

to the company, there will be a time to question and make suggestions.

When starting a new job, take some time to quietly sit in the back of the room and observe the work culture. That initial period of observation is essential if you are to succeed. If upon entering a workplace you seem very proud of your past accomplishments and want people to accept you because of them, you create a very poor, possibly irreversible, first impression. Top managers should tell their new employees to do nothing but observe the company's culture initially. This early period of being both attentive and modest – when all you do is listen, observe, and place yourself below everyone else – is the foundation of your success. If you are a passionate observer and an active listener, you can achieve all the success you can possibly handle.

Being attentive works in any workplace situation. It isn't a unique idea that as a new employee, you should make an effort to understand your new environment. The work culture in Canada places a great deal of value on humility, and failure to adapt to this is considered arrogance. For newcomers, understanding that not fitting in here is arrogance may seem a little odd and even surprising. This is because what Canadians see as arrogance is interpreted differently in most cultures. In most cultures, arrogance simply means snobbishness. Well the meaning is similar in Canada, but is extended to imply an unwillingness to adapt to the status quo.

In newcomers, arrogance can be seen as the following:

1. You have been here for a while, but your language skills are still weak. People may assume that you don't care about improving your language skills or that you are not good at setting goals for yourself.

2. You start a new job and immediately *stop* learning your new language. This shows you learned just enough to get the job – in other words, that making money is more important to you than fitting into the culture.

3. You speak your first language around the office with others who speak it too. People may feel you are talking about them.

4. You only watch TV programs broadcast in your first language, and prefer to read the news from your homeland. If you don't watch Canadian movies or TV, or follow the local news, what can people talk to you about? You will seem disconnected and unconcerned about the culture you live in.

5. You make no effort to remember the names of actors, athletes, musicians, or newsmakers, etc. Names are important, especially of those people who have worked hard to have their names recognized.

6. You interrupt people when they talk. To some of you, interrupting may seem like a sign of respect and show your interest in the conversation, but this isn't true in Canada.

7. You talk about your part-time job as a "survival job." Remember that many people do these jobs for a living, and it is disrespectful for you to call it a survival job.

8. You refer to your country of origin as "back home." This may imply that you would rather be there.

9. You fail to set your own goals. Don't wait for people to tell you what to do, where to work, what to study, and how best to learn the language. Do these things yourself and *for* yourself – set your own goals.

10. You are unfamiliar with the ten rules in this book. You need to be aware of the cultural expectations that exist where you live.

As you can see, the two lists may overlap. Even for some people who were born and raised here, new workplaces can still feel like a distant culture. And there are many more examples; I am sure you could add a lot more to these lists.

So, how do we come across as not arrogant? Well, the answer is very obvious from the lists above: try not to make mistakes – I know this is asking a lot, but people here tend to be a little judgmental, so people who constantly make mistakes may appear reckless and unpredictable. Above all, and as I have already suggested, don't try to appear to be more special than others. Control those impulses to show your uniqueness, especially if you are extremely talented; people will respect your humbleness. Notice how the great Canadian hockey players talk so modestly at press conferences. They talk about the team, not themselves.

If you're not careful, your colleagues may look at you and wonder who you are to think you are better than others. Who are you to not follow the rules that everyone else has to? In fact, if you do anything that doesn't uphold the status quo, you may be regarded as arrogant and maybe a little too unreasonable. And as the next chapter explores, knowing how you are perceived by those you work with is really important.

Self-reflection – How Are You Perceived?

In the Canadian workplace, you're considered reckless if you don't pay attention to your colleagues' feelings or how your behaviour affects them. Do you know how you are perceived? This exercise asks you to take an honest look at yourself and think about how others see you.

Consider the following scene:

Two children, Jacob and Sam, are kicking a ball back and forth near a lake. As you might expect the ball ends up in the water where neither child can reach it. Both children are upset because the game has abruptly finished. Jacob says:

"It isn't fair. Why did it have to go in the water? It could have bounced and gone anywhere! Why, of all places, did it have to go into the water? Stupid lake – you ruined our game!"

To which Sam replies:

"I think it was a mistake to play near the water. We should have known this would happen. We should have played somewhere else – we only have ourselves to blame."

Which child are you? Are you Jacob, who blames the lake, that ever-present natural force that is much like an established culture? Do you do that instead of identifying how your own poor decisions resulted in the end of the game?

Or are you Sam, who looks inward and reflects on the notion that we cannot change nature/culture, but we can change how we adapt to it? We have to be open to adapting to circumstances, not having those circumstances adapt to us.

The point is this: Would you swim against a strong river current? No, because it is completely arrogant to assume you can defeat the river. Well, imagine Canadian workplace culture, or any workplace culture anywhere in the world, as the river. Do you want to be the one swimming against the current while others watch you from the shore? Imagine what is going through their minds. Do you honestly think that going against the current helps you become successful in your career?

Rule 5:
Be Self-Perceptive and Proactive

When it comes to trying to fit in and not stand apart, there are many things to consider, and as I mentioned, fashion plays a major part. You really should note how colleagues are dressing. What's fashionable elsewhere may not be fashionable here. If you are a newcomer, try to abandon former trends and dress according to the workplace's norms. If you are an immigrant, what's fashionable at home may not be fashionable here.

Attempting to bring that fashion here sooner, by wearing it, may be regarded as arrogant and out of touch with the status quo. Fashions are different across the globe. If you go to job interviews wearing what is fashionable in your former country, you may send the wrong message, perhaps that you are a trendsetter. In Canada, being seen as a trendsetter isn't always a positive thing. Success is often established by being more of a trend follower. It shows you have respect for the status quo and that you want to be a part of the team.

In Canada, followers make the best leaders. Confused? Don't be. Followers are leaders in a conflict-averse culture. If we want to keep the peace, we make every effort to conform. This shows respect for others because it sends a signal that says, "Hey, we're the same, so we really know how we think. We can have a safe, conflict-free relationship."

However, others might say, "I am who I am, and I don't care what anyone thinks because I'm not here to make other people happy." This attitude may hurt them in the Canadian workplace. People who do this send a message that they think they are better than others, and they are beyond the rules. They may feel fine speaking their minds whenever they want to. Really, they are just standing out. They become their own worst enemies because others may even start to avoid them.

Apart from arrogance, your size and body language also play an important part in how you are perceived in the workplace. For example, tall people should try to appear a little less overwhelming. Canadians have difficulty with a large presence. Large or tall people, when entering a room, should be more conscious of the effect of their size, especially when others are sitting. They also need to speak softly and limit their gestures.

It's worth keeping in mind that, in a conflict-averse culture, people are always alert to any form of aggression. They notice everything you do. If you are tall and you walk in for a job interview and greet the receptionist by spreading your arms across the counter while towering over her, you are sending a very aggressive message.

Also, be very mindful that you need to be in sync with another person in your body language to show empathy. It is a good idea to mimic the other person's gestures to show you really understand how she is feeling. For example, if someone is talking energetically and raising her eyebrows in excitement, you should also raise your eyebrows. Also, think of body language in other terms as well. For example, try not to be the person who always reaches a door first. It may seem polite some of the time, depending on the situation, but monitor your behaviour. If you are in a restaurant having lunch with colleagues, are you always the first to reach the door? This could suggest that you feel you are the leader of the group. You may not be aware of your behaviour, but others may start noticing that you see yourself as the leader or as someone more important.

Realize that when you live in a culture in which people communicate indirectly, your body language is being observed at all times, even at a distance. For example, if you are standing in a line at the bank, all the tellers can see you being impatient and uncomfortable. They may have already determined that you are going to be rude, so they are defensive and anxious before you even approach them or start to talk.

Additionally, when you are attending a workplace training course in which you will be put into groups with other attendees, consider the following: First of all, for every session, be on time and be prepared. Second, be an active participant to show you are serious about your course. Third, stay off your computer or phone during the session – it shows the instructor and your colleagues respect. Why is this important? Later, your group may be broken up into smaller task groups, and all of the attendees will be hoping that they won't be put into groups with those who are late, uninterested, and disrespectful. The tension will already be rising almost immediately after the groups are formed. Always assume you are being watched at all times. And ask yourself: How am I being perceived?

I already mentioned that being tall affects others in a room, but your demeanour does too. Being too cheerful suggests that you are not working hard enough. By contrast, appearing tired disrupts the workplace atmosphere because it looks as if you cannot handle your job. In fact, it's insulting to tell people they look tired. If people say that to you, they may be trying to say, "You look as if you cannot handle pressure in your life." Establish a middle ground between not looking too cheerful and not appearing tired or overworked.

Also always be more interested in hearing about the other person's life and plans than discussing your own – follow Rule 1. If you always try to listen more than you talk, you will appear empathetic and understanding. People will feel that you are easy to talk to, and that is key to making a good first impression.

The first impressions you make at your new job will be the basis of the lasting perception people have of you. For example, on the first day, don't introduce yourself to everyone in the office. Stay quiet in the lunchroom during breaks. Wait for others to approach you first – be modest.

When people do approach you, try to downplay your position a little. Instead, show interest in what they have to say. Remember you are new, so try to show respect for the people who have been working there for a while. Listen to what they have to say and don't talk about yourself so much. In short, during the first month or so, act as though you are a guest in their home. After that time, people will want to get to know you more.

Some people make the mistake of thinking that during a first contact, you should show how much you have in common with the other person or persons. In fact, behaving with humility and putting the other person first gains the respect of colleagues. It is a carefully cultivated skill that separates those in top positions from those in entry-level positions.

Interestingly enough, problems sometimes arise when two people, both conscious of the importance of putting others first, meet. What do you do when both parties want to put the other person first? Consider their position in the workplace hierarchy. If they are your superiors, allow them to control the conversation. If you are their superior, you should keep the upper hand. Change the topic if necessary. Weather is always a nice fallback.

In the end, knowing how people perceive you helps you to adapt more successfully. Those who are a little stubborn and resent the status quo often have the hardest time because what others think doesn't matter to them. They just do their own thing. How can they change?

Worse still are those who know they are not conforming but refuse to accept reality. They may find themselves swimming against the current, wondering why they are not getting anywhere, and blaming the current for their lack of progress. Like Jacob on page 37, they need to have an honest conversation with themselves, one in which they ask, "What can I do to be a bit more empathetic and a bit more of a team player?"

Does this kind of person sound familiar? Well, you can swim against the current if you like, but this book is just trying to help you see that if you constantly run into obstacles with people at work, you eventually have to realize that the whole company isn't wrong. When your colleagues don't share your cynicism, don't just assume that they are part of the problem. When does the finger you point at everyone else finally point at you? Be self-perceptive and proactive.

Self-reflection – How Ready Are You?

Without a doubt, understanding how you are perceived and having the courage to make the changes necessary to fit in increases your chances of success. But are you ready to adapt or fit in? Ask yourself:

1. Do you care how people perceive you?
2. Do you feel it is important to be a follower?
3. Do you want people to perceive you as a team player?

Or

1. Do you think it is important to have a different or unique style?
2. Do feel it is important to be a trendsetter?
3. Do you not care what others think of you?

If you answered yes to the first three questions, you probably make a solid effort to be diplomatic and find ways to solve problems with like-minded individuals.

On the other hand, if the first three questions made you uncomfortable and you said "yes" to the last three, you are probably struggling at work. If you are about to enter a new workplace, be aware that your success really depends on whether you are perceived positively by your colleagues.

In the next chapter you'll see that your interaction during meetings is the ultimate test in determining how easy you are to work with and how conscious you are of the rules. Here, everything you are and all that you believe is on display revealing whether you fit in or stand apart.

Rule 6:
Be Diplomatic in Meetings

Another aspect that makes life hard for Canadians in the workplace is the meeting. People from some cultures with assertive communication styles may see meetings as opportunities to showcase their strengths. They may see meetings as a practical means of getting things decided as quickly as possible. These people don't mind saying, "I disagree with you," or "I don't think so." They speak directly to get to the point faster and come to a conclusion more efficiently. They have no problem being confronted in this manner as well. They see this type of exchange as honest, open, and necessary. After the meeting, they feel they can put negative talk behind them and feel good about coming to a solution.

In a conflict-averse culture, this direct way of talking may be considered rude. To say to someone, "I see what you mean, but..." or "I completely disagree with you," or "I don't think that's a good idea," or even starting rebuttals with *no* is seen as a little aggressive and not empathetic. Sentences that start with *no*, for example, "No, what I meant was..." or "No, I don't think so," create a negative vibe in the discussion.

Most interpersonal textbooks will tell you that there is nothing wrong with a little conflict, and it leads to healthy relationships. True, but for Canadians, conflict in the workplace often happens when all else fails. When the other person isn't reading the non-verbal cues and the truth has to be spelled out, this is considered awkward.

Consider the following example. Imagine a colleague is sending emails that are a little too direct and can be perceived as rude. You approach her and say:

"Hey, I got your email today."

You take a deep breath, make eye contact and hesitate a little:

"Yeah, you are really straightforward in emails."

You smile slightly, showing a little concern. Her response would probably be:

"Oh, was it a little too strongly worded?"

However, she might ignore all your signs of discomfort and say:

"Yeah, well I always like to get to the point."

But she has failed to *get* the point. If so, you might say:

"Yeah, some might see that as getting to the point."

There would be hesitation in your voice, a slowdown in your speech, and reduced eye contact as you indirectly asserted your point.

But she still might not understand your non-verbal cues, and may ask why you don't just say, in words, what's on your mind. That would provoke you into an impatient reaction that may sound like this:

"Perhaps you should be a little more careful about how you word your emails because they sound rude."

Since she favours direct talk, she would feel relieved and grateful that you just said it straight out. In her mind, the matter would be out in the open and being dealt with. However, the indirect communicator reacts differently. Are you direct communicators ready for what is coming next?

The direct communicator leaves this exchange feeling refreshed that she had an open and honest dialogue, whereas the more indirect communicator feels taxed emotionally. What happens next is that the indirect communicator makes up their mind to have less or little to do with the person who needs things said so directly. In a conflict-averse culture, which depends on indirect communication patterns, people tend to avoid those who don't communicate the same way they do.

In meetings, be especially careful how you express yourself. Meetings are where Canadians and newcomers alike really have to ask themselves if they are seeing the bigger workplace picture. Some newcomers may believe that if they can just master the language, they will be fine. However, if they neglect to notice everything else – the non-verbal cues – they may miss the intended messages and become frustrated.

Frustration is natural to anyone moving to a new culture. In the first stage, everything is new and fascinating; everyone is polite. In the next stage, you realize how little you actually know and how people around you are expecting you to adapt and fit in. That can be a challenge, but it helps to take stock, reflect on what you're doing and then make an effort to fit into the greater picture. The fact is people often get promoted because they fit in.

In some assertive cultures, the opinions of the decision makers are the most important ones. If the bosses like you, they can promote you – it is their choice. They got to where they are because of their bold and unique personalities, and are expected to lead accordingly. They make decisions that may not make perfect sense to you but that ultimately benefit the organization.

In less assertive cultures the *wa* must be maintained above all else. *Wa* is a Japanese term meaning "harmony and peace." Japanese workplaces, also known for indirect communication, see maintaining the *wa* as everyone's responsibility. Everyone must be cheerful and polite at all times. A person doesn't want to be responsible for bringing that *wa* down. Canadian workplaces are similar in this regard. There is a *wa* that needs to be maintained, and that can make meetings tough. Words must be measured carefully, and respect for others comes first.

People in these less assertive, conflict-averse cultures really need to be aware of the *wa* and put the feelings of others first. They are not simply trying to be more polite; they are trying to avoid a conflict, which is the real goal. Before you respond, imagine what it feels like if someone uses negative terminology with you. If you can deliver your message without using such terminology, you avoid potential conflicts.

In the end, what people from cultures with indirect communication styles may view as polite, people from more assertive cultures may view as insincere. And the opposite is also true. So what do we do if we are from one culture but working in another? Well again, "When in Rome..." Every culture is distinct and impressive, but there are pros and cons you need to face when working and living in any of them.

The point here isn't to say that one type of culture is more polite than another. We just want to understand why people from cultures where indirect communication prevails tend to think of the feelings of others first before speaking their minds. Politeness may well be a factor. Generally though, in cultures with indirect communication, considering others' feelings is simply a necessary way to protect yourself from damaging workplace relationships. For this reason, people in these cultures struggle with meetings from time to time.

Because of the indirect and polite patterns of communicating that exist in the Canadian workplace, successful meetings take time and effort. People need to be careful how they listen and respond to others. Meetings can be particularly delicate because a mistake with an individual colleague is one thing, but having a confrontation with that person in an open meeting before the entire staff could be devastating.

Many Canadian business leaders often feel frustrated because their employees are overly cautious in meetings, making them unproductive. I have often been asked about the reason for caution, and the answer is simple: Canadians are cautious in meetings because if you push someone too far, you may have an enemy for life. In general, they judge direct behaviour as a sign of rudeness, and once they determine that someone doesn't understand the social rules of engagement, they avoid and dislike them. In short, maintaining the *wa* may be more important in meetings than achieving a final resolution.

In the workplace, Canadians are very cautious in both social events and meetings. They tend to show negativity through non-verbal cues, not words. In a meeting, if I were to disagree with you, I might say, "I see your point, and it has value. What I am wondering is this..." No "buts" and nothing negative would be said, and I would be easy on you. However, I might look down and shift my papers a bit to show that I don't like the idea much.

If you find a Canadian colleague being blunt with you, it could be because he has lost respect for you and no longer wishes to put your feelings first. Try to be more introspective and figure out what you did to offend that person. Also, try to make an effort to talk to him. Perhaps you can both work toward a solution to improve your communication in the future.

Meetings are different in workplaces that communicate in direct versus non-direct ways. In cultures that communicate directly, you can sit down and get right to business, even if you don't know the other people's points of view. But, in a culture with more indirect communication, more pre-meeting lobbying is needed.

Here unexpected meetings without agendas tend to be unproductive.

Agendas should be sent out well in advance so that participants have time to discover the opinions of others and know where they stand relative to each other before the meeting. The meeting will be friendlier if participants are already aware of who supports a certain view and why. This helps them temper their perspectives and be prepared to switch sides if need be without losing face. The concept here is simple: in a conflict-averse culture, predictability maintains calm and strengthens relationships. When events are spontaneous or unplanned, people get tense and meetings don't go well.

Meetings in Canada need to be treated with a great deal of respect. Never interrupt other people when they are talking. Focus completely on whoever is doing the talking – conversations taking place while another person is speaking are considered very rude. And make sure you are not checking your phone or your computer, as no one will ever assume you are doing these things for the purpose of the meeting – unless, of course, you have been asked to take minutes or research a point for the meeting.

Never come late to meetings, and don't ask anyone what you missed. The chair of the meeting will tell you about the meeting if he wants to show that he knows why you are late and is fine with it. In the end, the chair of the meeting, usually your supervisor, is telling you about the kind of relationship you have, and that leads us to Rule 7

Self-reflection – Are You Promotable?

The opinion your supervisors have of you comes partly from how you conduct yourself in meetings. Ask yourself a few questions to determine whether their opinion is favourable.

1. Do you try to fit in and follow meeting procedures without complaining?
2. Do you have a reputation for empathy in meetings and around the workplace in general?
3. Are you a constructive contributor?
4. Do you get your point across agreeably, without offending anyone?
5. Do you show respect for others by being on time, not interrupting, and not getting distracted?

The Canadian workplace requires a lot from you both mentally and physically, and you need to spend as much energy maintaining workplace relationships as you do carrying out the duties you were hired for.

Along with that your relationship with your supervisor also needs to be carefully cultivated. Never take that relationship for granted, no matter how close you feel it is. So learn to see things from your supervisor's perspective and try to be the best employee you can be.

Rule 7:
Build Strong Rapport with Supervisors

We have all heard supervisors say, "My door is always open," or "Call if you have any problems." The question is just how wide is that door actually open? How big do the problems have to be before we can actually walk through it? In truth the supervisor doesn't really want you walking through that door unless it's to tackle a problem that's beyond your authority and capability to resolve without their help. So you need to be careful that you're not asking for help with a problem your supervisor thinks you should be able to deal with yourself.

To build a good relationship with your supervisor, you don't have to tell him what you are doing well; let him hear about you through praise from other employees, or let him see it for himself through your work. That is how a supervisor likes to learn about you. He likes to know that you can solve your own problems without complaints. He likes to know that you are a strong team player that your colleagues can depend on. Making cheerful small talk with your supervisor about the hard work you do is sometimes helpful, but this is not what advances your relationship. Your reputation, as reported through indirect channels, builds your relationship.

In our indirect culture you are much more likely to be successful in a job when your reputation among your colleagues is favourable. Remember that supervisors like conflict-free environments. So if your colleagues show that they respect you and like working with you, then it's easier for your supervisor to promote you. In Canada, supervisors respect those who bring the fewest problems - *bring solutions, not problems*. You become more valuable when you can solve your own problems.

Another common mistake is to expect your supervisor to keep you informed about certain matters, especially those pertaining to the upper management's strategies. Supervisors, by the very nature of their job, can't tell you everything, often because they're bound by company policies. If you feel that your supervisor isn't being completely honest with you, just remember there are certain things they cannot tell you. How should you react to this? Keep in mind that you may not be seeing the whole picture, just your part of it. Your supervisor's decisions are based on that bigger picture; a picture that they may not be allowed to show you.

Supervisors typically make decisions very carefully and only after thorough consideration of all the stakeholders involved. Let's look at an example. Imagine that you hear that company policy states your boss has the authority to promote you without going through a formal open posting or interview process. Would you approach him and ask him to promote you directly? In some cultures, a supervisor would use that policy to bring in whoever he wanted, but in a Canadian workplace, it's much different. A supervisor here would still go through the whole hiring process to make other concerned groups feel respected and appreciated. Talking directly to the supervisor about your promotion only makes you look out of step with how things are done in Canada.

Similarly, if you constantly complain to your supervisor that members of your staff aren't being safe, it doesn't show your commitment to safety but rather that you're not doing your job well enough. If your group isn't being safe, your supervisor may assume that either they don't respect you or that you don't communicate well.

In the end, when your supervisor tells you the door is always open, it is – but only for very extreme situations that are completely out of your control, like criminal behaviour such as theft and sexual harassment. Other issues such as pay or working hours may also need to be discussed. In other words, if you have to knock on that door, make sure it's about something you have no authority to make a decision on. That is the only time the door is really always open. If something falls under your authority to fix it, *then fix it*.

By the way, when it comes to money, always have that conversation face-to-face; money talk is never well received over emails or phone calls.

Generally speaking, becoming valued by your supervisor isn't about knocking on his door; it's about maintaining strong rapport with colleagues and being a strong and independent problem solver.

Building rapport with people isn't always easy, and it

takes time. Saying no is never easy, especially to supervisors and particularly when you start a new job. Supervisors just like to hear yes. In most cases, especially in the beginning of a job, yes is the only answer you can really give. When you are new and the supervisor asks you to take on a certain role you are not necessarily prepared for, you just have to say, "Yeah, sure I can do that."

If you start off by saying, "Well, that's not what we agreed on, I thought I would be doing this," you will make a bad first impression. Colleagues may also find your attitude odd – especially those who have been there a while.

Imagine that you are new to the company and there are two shifts – morning and afternoon. You prefer to work in the afternoon, but are scheduled to work in the morning. What do you do? Nothing – just respond with "thank you." When you have more seniority, you may have a little more room for negotiation. But if you are new, be careful about showing anxiety or displeasure about how things are done in your workplace, it could be perceived as arrogance.

If you have been working at a company for a while and you suddenly get a new supervisor, start rebuilding that rapport all over again. Don't describe your relationship expectations to him – that is arrogance. Remember, your supervisor, not you, determines when trust between you both has been established.

Build credibility by always being the person the supervisor depends on. Once you have established that credibility and demonstrated your loyalty to the company, you can then start to feel comfortable turning things down.

When do you know you have reached that point? Well, you've reached it when your supervisor likes talking to you and starts giving you choices about your work. When you notice those *quality time* opportunities with your supervisor developing naturally, you will have more flexibility to say no to certain things without any repercussions (later, in Rule 10, we'll talk about the importance of knowing *when* to say no).

Transitioning into a new position takes at least a year, so don't expect that flexibility too soon. First you have to become the person your supervisor really depends on. Having said this, I reiterate: Your success in the workplace depends almost entirely on how you are perceived by your colleagues. We'll discuss rapport building with colleagues in Rule 8.

Self-reflection – Are Colleagues on Your Team?

To get promoted or gain your supervisor's favour, you need to have good relationships with your colleagues. Some people think they only need to impress their supervisor but, remember, she probably got to where she is by first winning over her colleagues. She worked within her workplace culture, avoided adding to her supervisor's workload and gained the respect of her colleagues. Promotion was a reward for her ability to solve problems, not create them. If you want to advance your career, consider these questions:

1. Do you realize that supervisors find out about you from your colleagues?
2. Do you realize that promotion depends almost entirely on your colleagues' feelings about you?
3. Do you know how you are perceived?
4. Do you know what your colleagues are telling your supervisor?
5. Do you think your colleagues' approval is important to your success?
6. Do you like intimidating your colleagues?
7. Do you like to win and show you are better than your colleagues?
8. Do you think you're better at your job than your colleagues are?
9. Do you see yourself as an indispensable team member?

The point is if you aren't following the rules, and trying to be a good colleague, then you are probably being your own saboteur and creating obstacles to your own success!

Rule 8:
Build Strong Rapport with Colleagues

Making friends with colleagues can be a little easier than winning over your supervisor, but you still need to be careful. Build strong rapport with your colleagues, but not too soon. Usually, it takes at least six months before people really start to get comfortable with you. Don't push for good rapport to happen earlier. In other words, don't come into the office every day, shaking everyone's hands and saying good morning. Be a little less outgoing.

Let people approach you when they are ready. Research shows that they will need a little time. Scientists who observed primates in the wild found that it took many months for the animals to become used to their scent and approach them. The relationship then changed and the scientists were finally accepted. They cannot just grab the baby gorilla from the mother on the first day and say, "Hey, cute little fellow!" What would happen? Well, the same thing – a negative reaction – would happen if you did the equivalent of this in the workplace. In short, *be a scientist!* Observe everything before you consider how to interact. Be open to all things said and unsaid. Watch how people at work dress and how the culture functions.

In Canada, workplaces are tricky. Be careful about what you say and how you say it. Be diplomatic at all times. You need to *not* stand out. Be empathetic. Avoid being seen as arrogant because it can take a long time to reverse that impression. Most of all, be aware that everything you say or do can get back to your supervisor.

There are several things you can do to build better rapport:

First, try to identify and understand the different personality types you work with. Since you can't change other people, it's in your best interests to understand and adapt to them a little – it will make your interactions with others more successful. Be a keen observer and try to read between the lines to discover what people are really trying to say.

Second, don't take advantage of colleagues who possess certain skills. For example, try to take notes when a technical expert explains something in case you need the same information later. Don't ask the same questions over and over because you'll appear unconcerned or even lazy.

Third, when you are participating in teams, be agreeable and open to compromise. Try to avoid conflict. Listen carefully when they are talking and remember to use some polite and indirect language when you talk to them.

Fourth, know *how* to be agreeable. When you are asked to do something, people like it when you *agree to it with a reason*. For example, if you are asked to do some research, respond with, "That's sounds great! I know just where to start getting the information." If you were to simply say, "Sure, I'll do that," it might sound as if you're not very interested in the idea. So try to agree with a reason – this makes it less likely that people will feel they are pushing you into something.

Fifth, in a culture that puts others first, negative criticism and bad news are offered in indirect ways – through non-verbal messages rather than negative words. If you find yourself in a situation like this, paying attention to non-verbal cues can make things a lot easier on you. If the person you're talking to takes a deep breath, then recognize that hesitation in their body language as a foreboding to bad news or criticism. Let's take a closer look at an example of this last one:

Emma approaches Kelly with an idea that Kelly doesn't completely like:

"Hey Kelly, I have an idea that I think you would like! What if we change the logo from an apple to a banana?"

Kelly takes a deep breath and looks carefully at the banana logo. She tilts her head a little, takes another deep breath, avoids eye contact and responds slowly and softly:

"All right, Emma... I see what you are trying to do here... and it is a good idea."

Kelly sighs a little and continues:

"What I am thinking is that the client may want to stick with the apple because of the wishes of the company's founder... the banana does look good though."

Kelly then looks up, raises her eyebrows, makes eye contact, and says to Emma:

"Perhaps we can keep working with the apple, and if the client changes her mind..."

Kelly looks down again, focuses on the logo, tilts her head a bit more, and pauses for Emma to step in and affirm that perhaps the banana isn't the best idea, at which point Emma says:

"Yeah, okay, I see your point. I suppose we should just keep working with the apple."

Emma looks down at the logo and isn't making eye contact. Meanwhile, Kelly takes a breath, and responds encouragingly:

"Well it is a nice perspective... nice work on this. Maybe we can show the clients next week and see what they think."

Emma makes eye contact with a kind of "it's-up-to-you" expression, her eyebrows raised.

"Yes okay. For now, though, I'll get back to work on this apple logo, maybe I can make a few changes to make this closer to what the client really wants."

Kelly brings the discussion to an end:

"Okay, sounds great – nice work! Let's talk soon!"

This is how a conversation takes place when both people involved try to put the feelings of the other person first. In this case, Kelly doesn't want to insult Emma or upset her by rejecting her idea, but she has to convey clearly that the banana logo won't work. Emma, in turn has to pick up on Kelly's non-verbal cues if the two of them are to find their way out of this dilemma. Both sides win here, and maintain their respect for each other.

The way Kelly and Emma behave reveals their respect for each other and the workplace. This kind of empathetic communication, which uses a lot of non–verbal hints, may seem indirect to the point of dishonesty for some, but it is what is expected in workplaces across Canada. Those who master this indirect way of giving and receiving messages, tend to succeed in their careers and become respected by all who know them.

In Canada, when we are giving negative feedback, we tend to start with positive news. It acts as a buffer for the bad news coming next. This is a fine approach. When you start with the positive, avoid saying "but" before the negative. You could say, "You did a great job on that project... you know, I am just wondering if you could have handled that situation with the client a little better." Starting with the positive is a good way to get to the negative.

However, if you know you will be giving bad news after the good news, your non- verbal cues should let the person receiving it know this is happening. If you start off too cheerfully, you make the other person feel too comfortable and relaxed. This is unfair, as you are setting him up for a fall. He will feel cheated or betrayed if you suddenly go from being cheerful to stern.

When delivering bad news after the good news, start with a neutral, almost serious, tone and a slight yet genuine smile. Your tone and body language (neutral eyebrows, for example), still somewhat positive, allow the person on the receiving end to anticipate the bad news. He will respect the buffer, but won't get too comfortable. This is the respectful approach for giving this sort of feedback.

Sometimes, you may need to deal with staff members in other departments. Bear in mind that the administrative assistants in any department need to be respected. They are often responsible for a lot of day-to-day operations, and they may feel that they are really the ones doing all the work of those operations. Treat them with respect and show them how much you appreciate their hard work.

Never treat them as your own personal assistants. When you ask them to do something for you, they will seem happy to do it. But after you leave they will resent you asking them to do something you could have done yourself. Here's an example. In your company, most people book appointments through Microsoft Outlook. Since, you're not familiar with that program you ask the administrative assistant to book an appointment for you. She may book the appointment in good humour, but she and those in her department will wonder why you didn't do it yourself. Remember that the administrative assistants work for the company and the boss. Notice how the leader of that department talks to them - cautiously and empathetically. You need to do the same.

And never be in an urgent state when approaching support staff for help. Always buffer your conversation by using a pleasant greeting and a little small talk when you approach people for things you need. Never get to business right away, but make time to exchange a few pleasantries. This ensures that you have a reputation around the company as a polite and respectful individual. Remember, everyone you work with is your colleague, and you should treat people as you wish to be treated.

In short, always be a keen observer. Remember that sometimes the true message is in people's body language and what people don't say, rather than in their words. Be open to receiving messages from every direction, and in every form. The bottom line is simple: in a culture with an indirect communication style, things, especially bad news or criticism, will be said indirectly.

Self-reflection – What Creates Strong Rapport?

Try to think of your most successful colleague, someone who has developed excellent relationships with their peers. Now ask yourself these questions:

1. What did she do to gain respect from others?
2. How does she treat you and other colleagues?
3. How is she perceived by those she works with?
4. How is she perceived by her supervisor?
5. How does she deliver feedback?
6. How well does she listen? Does she listen more than she talks?
7. Is she empathetic?
8. How does she treat junior staff?
9. Why do people like her?
10. Does she communicate respectfully with everyone?

The fact is, her success in the workplace is achieved by hard work on both her job and her relationships – she works hard, and she knows what to work hard on!

When you work at a job, you actually need to work hard at two jobs, the one you are hired to do and the one that requires you to form strong interpersonal relationships with your colleagues. Yes you need to be great at your technical specialty, but if you can't get along with colleagues your dreams of gaining promotion, and your supervisor's respect, will be lost. Remember that there's always another employee ready to take your place. Your ability to fit in determines how successful you are going to be. So let's read on and see what it means to work hard to fit in.

Rule 9:
Work Hard at the Job AND at Fitting In

The key to being successful in the Canadian workplace is to never let yourself feel that you are indispensable; because once you do, things can start to fall apart. In the end, how hard you work determines how valuable you are, not how indispensable you feel.

Canadian culture is all about fitting in and giving people what they want and expect. Even if you graduate the top of your class, you are not guaranteed the job you want. Nothing matters except your ability to show that your personality and style fit the company culture. Making that happen takes work.

In a culture with an indirect communication style, bosses don't really promote you, your colleagues do. Because Canadian supervisors are exceptionally skilled at avoiding conflict, their hiring decisions and promotions may depend on how your colleagues feel about you. Even though your supervisor may like you, he won't promote you if you have a poor reputation among your colleagues. You may have talked to him in private, making a very strong case for your promotion. Maybe he said, "Yes, I think you would make a great new manager. When the opportunity arises, you are in!"

After such a conversation, you might feel your promotion is secure. And why wouldn't you? A trusted leader just told you so, right to your face. You might even go home and tell your family, and all of you might celebrate. At work you feel confident and super-charged; until you notice that the promotion isn't mentioned anymore. When asked, your supervisor reassures you it could still happen. But days turn into weeks and, "...oh my goodness!" Someone else gets promoted. What happened?

What happened was that your supervisor initially thought you would be a good choice, but after asking around the office, he realized that promoting you would equal new headaches for him. He asked your colleagues how they like working with you and how they would react to your promotion. And since you didn't get the promotion, you can guess what they replied. Depending on the company, he may also have asked the main receptionist about you because that receptionist has her finger on the pulse of the office. In truth, if anyone has a clear picture of how your promotion would affect office dynamics, the receptionist does. So, rather than telling you, your supervisor simply decided to let the topic slowly disappear. What could he say? "I would like to promote you, but no one here would like that."

In the Canadian workplace, the default approach is to avoid problems. And as frustrating and hurtful as not being promoted may be, you need to let it go. You gain nothing by pushing for advancement. If you were to say to your supervisor, "You promised me!" You, not the supervisor, would look like the troublemaker. By showing your anger, frustration, and lack of understanding, you simply confirm that everyone is right about you.

It's not easy to conform to any culture. Wherever you go, you'll have to make an effort to fit in, and it takes hard work. You need to learn the language, the culture, and how the people act. We all have a responsibility to conform to and be a part of that culture. The same goes for corporate culture.

When you enter a new company, what do you need to work hard at? First, observe the company culture and conform to it as best as you can. Going to a new job is a lot like going to someone's house for dinner. Would you keep your shoes on when no one else does? Would you start moving the pictures on the piano because you don't like the way they are placed? Would you talk about what a great cook you are while eating the dinner your host prepared for you? Would you insist on sitting in the best chair in the house? Would you dominate the conversation? Or would you listen more than you talk? Would it be more important for you to be interesting yourself or interested in others? Being the best guest you can be takes a lot of effort and dedication. So does being the best employee.

Always be aware that people are watching you very closely. Although you might have expertise and experience, perhaps years of it, remember that you are still being hired for your ability to fit in. Sometimes your expertise and experience is really just a bonus.

In the beginning, you will be given a certain grace period to adapt. After a while, if it appears you are not fitting in or making an effort to do so, you might fall out of favour with your colleagues and even your supervisor. Eventually, your one- year contract turns into your *only* year contract.

Success in any workplace is based on how well you understand and adapt to it. If you have no interest in it, you'll fail. If you feel superior to those around you, you'll fail. If you feel your way is best, you'll fail. If you think you can ignore the rules, you'll fail. The same is true in any workplace.

The Canadian workplace isn't better or worse than any other workplace in the world; it simply is different and has different rules. The rules here are simple, like anywhere else, and your success depends on how hard you work at following them.

The positive side to Canadian culture is what everyone can agree on: Canadians are peaceful, friendly, and polite people who shy away from conflict. This positive side is maintained through a collective compromise: *you need to fit in*. This is seen as a form of surrender for those who value individualism. But what can you do? If you're uncomfortable working in this type of environment, you can always become your own boss, start your own business, or look for companies that share your ideals and values. They are out there. Every day, more and more multinational companies set up offices in Canada. There are also companies started by entrepreneurs who didn't fit into conflict-averse workplaces. Therefore, you may simply need to be more selective if you wish to work in a place that accepts you for who you are.

Culture is what it is, and culture develops into what it is for many different reasons. There is no perfect culture, only negatives and positives. And we all have to work as hard as we can to contribute to the positives while we learn to deal with the negatives – *in a positive way*. Sometimes we prefer to look only at the positive aspects and ignore the negative ones, but we need to embrace and understand both.

Adapting to a culture is like starting a new relationship. You wouldn't begin a relationship thinking, "I like this person but there are a few things I don't like and need to change." You can't change people – look at how hard it is to change you! If you can't change yourself, what chance do you have of changing someone else? And if you can't change one person, what's the likelihood of changing an entire workplace? In other words, understand the work culture you are in and try to work with it, not against it.

Canadian work culture rewards those who make every effort to conform to, and be part of, the team. The fact is, Canadians are very hard working, both in their jobs and in building and maintaining relationships. If you step out the norms and decide to do your own thing, you do so potentially at your own risk.

For example, if you work for a company with a conservative dress code and you show up with green hair, expect your supervisor to start thinking about getting rid of you. If you insist on being the only one who wears a bow tie or bright red shoes, expect your colleagues to react negatively. Conforming isn't easy, but it is crucial. Fortunately there's an added bonus – fitting in brings the acceptance that leads to success.

Self-reflection – What Do You Work Hard On?

Hard work is all about how you contribute positively to your work environment. In any given culture, you contribute proactively by knowing the proper way of conducting yourself. There are rules you need to observe, and expectations you need to fulfill, in order to succeed. Take some time to reflect on the following questions:

1. Do you think that how well you perform your duties is primarily what leads to your promotion?
2. Do you think that showing colleagues your unique style will help you get ahead?
3. Do you think that your supervisor makes decisions without considering the opinions of others?
4. Do you think that you have a responsibility to adapt to a work culture? Or do you think that work culture has a responsibility to adapt to you?

By now, you should have come to a few conclusions about Canadian workplace culture. Generally speaking, people here are very hard working and you need to adjust to be successful. The conflict-averse workplace isn't the best place for everyone, and if you struggle with it, take a look around, there are workplaces with more assertive styles you may be a better fit for.

In the last rule, we reach the conclusion. There we find the answer to this question: When can you have more control and independence from supervisors and colleagues. *When* can you say no? The short answer is, only after you have demonstrated that you are a model fit.

Rule 10:
Know When to Say No

Saying no can be difficult when you are in a culture that judges you by how hard you work. So how do you say no? Well, in Canada, how you say no is less important than when you say no. The last kind of employee you want to be is one who can never be counted on for anything. Don't be someone who picks and chooses only what you want to do. When you start at a company, the supervisor will often ask you to do certain tasks or ask for volunteers. In most cases, this asking is really not a question. She only needs you to say yes or say, "I can volunteer for that – I enjoy that kind of activity" (remember to agree with a reason). Like your supervisor, your colleagues expect a high degree of cooperation, so try to help when asked.

So when do you say no? In the beginning, you don't. Often, those employees who work more hours or agree to take on extra work and volunteer for company functions become highly valued, whereas people who work only the minimum required hours become vulnerable to those yearly contracts. Being a new employee comes with a lack of life-work balance.

However, after a while, you can strategically say no to certain things. This happens after you have proven your loyalty to the company and have gone beyond the call of duty on more than one occasion.

One time, I had a student who was working for a moving company. One of his colleagues heard that there would be layoffs and suggested he take on more shifts. He followed the advice and breathed a sigh of relief when he later discovered that the two people who were laid off hadn't taken extra shifts. Given this example, you should volunteer to take on extra responsibilities.

Here's another example. An executive at a mid–sized trading company took exception to a comment I made about cutbacks targeting employees who don't volunteer, cooperate, or show enthusiasm and loyalty. She claimed all of her company's employees were given equal consideration during recent cutbacks. But when asked how many of those laid-off employees had been volunteering, accepting requests and showing consistent, enthusiastic loyalty, she had to admit these issues had come up.

Your ability to show that you are very reliable through your hard work builds you tenure at your company, providing you with the job security you are looking for. Eventually, you will find yourself in a pretty secure situation and you can escape certain responsibilities, but to build that kind of relationship takes time.

So how should you feel when it becomes clear that you are not yet in a place to say "yes" or "no"? How should you feel about your work-life balance being subject to the whim of others? Well, you just need to let it go. Just wait and see, and while you do, take a good look at yourself and how you are being perceived by your colleagues. You should be able to get a sense of when your colleagues are starting to trust you. They will start to ask you more about yourself and show curiosity about your life and interests. If you never sense that this is happening, ask yourself what you are missing. How are you being perceived? To take control of your career, it is important to gain the respect of everyone you work with. Once that control is achieved, you can determine your work-life balance as you see fit.

Canada's culture is unique, just as other cultures are. As with every culture, there are upsides and downsides but dwelling on the negative is useless. We should try to be more accepting and adaptable. What choice do we have? If we work here, how does it help to go completely against the status quo? You need to be perceived well by the people you work with first; later, once you've achieved that, you'll be able to choose what you do.

Canadians have to work hard to conform to the status quo. The sooner people realize that, the more success they are likely to achieve. Some are stubborn, direct, and neglectful of the rules, struggling against the accepted way of doing things. They can often become disillusioned and paranoid, feeling everyone is out to get them. Colleagues smile at them but want very little to do with them. They work hard and are promised promotions from well-intentioned supervisors or managers, but promotions never come. They feel betrayed and lied to. They feel surrounded by dishonest people who, on the surface, smile and say one thing, but then turn around and do another.

What would make their lives easier? They should take a look at themselves to see if they are doing enough to fit in. They need to be a little less brazen and a little more careful at mapping out their course, while always considering the feelings of others before they act. They should be supportive and agreeable when people ask them to do things. In other words, they should set their goals and work toward them, so they can be just as successful here as anywhere else.

Political and business leaders in Canada get to the top by following the rules and doing their best to fit in; not by challenging the system but by knowing it very well. They all started at the bottom, accepting what was asked of them. Saying yes is the first step. Building rapport with your colleagues is the next. After that, you have to cultivate the respect of your supervisor. From there, certain opportunities will start to arise and you will have more flexibility to say no to certain things.

In Canada, following a process and knowing the traditional approach is the first order of business. Following predictable, established standards helps to eliminate the possibility of conflict. Uncharted waters means uncertainty, and with uncertainty comes the possibility of conflict.

Even though in your heart you may know that you are truly talented at what you do, remind yourself that others are just as talented or perhaps even more so. This thinking encourages you to work harder at building stronger workplace relationships. Even after you work extremely hard to build your reputation, you still need to present yourself modestly as a person who isn't irreplaceable.

Doing so makes people respect you even more and is the way you get to the top of your profession.

People who feel that they're more important than others get too comfortable responding "No" or "Yes, but..." when things are asked of them. Remember, there is a time when you can negotiate, and that time usually comes after you've demonstrated how hard you work.

To succeed in any culture, you have to have realistic expectations. In other words, things are expected of you that you may not be comfortable with or prepared for. I am speaking about the day-to-day interactions people have with each other in the workplace: the simple rules of engagement. In the Canadian workplace, you must avoid conflict, and your ability to fit in demonstrates that you respect the culture. And fitting in all depends on being willing to look inwards and see what other people see when they look at you.

Self-reflection – Are You Willing to Adapt?

Well, we have almost come to the end. We have looked at the ten rules no one really tells us about, and I hope you now have a clearer picture of what to expect in the Canadian workplace. With that clearer picture, it's time to consider how willing you are to adapt:

1. Do you think the ten rules in this book are unreasonable?
2. Do you think you don't need to change yourself a little to fit in?
3. Do you feel people should accept you, even though you're at odds with some of the rules?

Or

1. Do you think these rules are reasonable?
2. Can you make a few changes to fit in a better?
3. Would you put others first if it makes the workplace more harmonious?

If you find yourself saying yes to the first three, chances are you are still going to struggle a bit in the workplace. If you said no to the first three questions and yes to the last three, then you are poised for success in the Canadian workplace.

The choice is yours. If you are committed to looking forward and *turning things around*, I invite you to read the final chapter that follows.

Turning Things Around

After reading this book, you might ask, "Okay, so I've made a few mistakes, broken a few of the rules, and noticed that I'm being perceived badly, so what do I do to turn things around?" The simple act of asking this question is really the first step to any real change.

What follows are a few ideas for turning things around. The good news is, the hard part is over. For many people, taking that first step of admitting that they could try a little harder is the most difficult step. The next part is basically just taking a series of small steps in the right direction.

Start by telling yourself that you are *not* always right; your colleagues, your boss, and the organization aren't wrong for maintaining the status quo. You are the one who is out of step with it. *You cannot change a culture or expect to be accepted if you don't follow its rules.*

Stay professional at work and try to improve your interpersonal skills. Make yourself more *other-oriented* by listening 80 percent of the time and talking only 20 percent of the time. Showing more interest in what other people have to say improves your relationships almost immediately. Also, try to be an active listener. When people are talking, ask more questions. And try to express more empathy in your body language by nodding or by showing on your face that you understand a person and perhaps feel for the situation she is in. In short, put yourself second in that conversation, and make other people feel that they are more important.

Take a look at your wardrobe in comparison to the standard way of dressing in your workplace. Make sure your wardrobe is professional and appropriate for your organization. In a conservative workplace, abandon *statement pieces* or a trendier style, which are fine for weekends or going out with friends. However, depending on the industry, some workplaces may have different expectations. In some industries such as music, fashion, or design, staff is expected to be more stylish. Whatever the case, remember that teamwork is an important part of the workplace, and how you dress tells people what you think about the team. If you dress above it or below it, you are out of sync with your colleagues.

Volunteer more at work. If events come up and the company needs volunteers, put your name in. Also, if your boss suddenly wants you to take on extra tasks, don't mention money – just do the work cheerfully. Taking on additional responsibilities without asking for money builds trust between you and your supervisor – he won't forget the sacrifices you make! So don't worry about money. Above all, volunteering for things shows that you have enthusiasm for your job and a close connection with your colleagues.

Make a habit of remembering people's names. And use those names when you talk to, or about, people. Everyone has a responsibility to do this. If you are not from Canada and you have a hard time remembering names here, make more of an effort. Try to mention a person's name a few times in your first conversation with him, and write his name down later and say it a few times. You'll be surprised how easy it can be if you make a little extra effort. Canadians born and raised here should also try to learn how to remember and pronounce the names of colleagues from other countries. It helps foster an environment of mutual respect.

Approach people with courtesy before you talk business. For example, start with a nice smile and say, "Good morning! How are you?" And when someone asks you, "How are you?" don't forget to respond with, "Good, and you?" This simple exchange sets the tone for the whole conversation that follows. Leave a little room for small talk before you get to business. For newcomers to Canada, pay more attention to local news and events so you are more prepared for these conversations.

When you are in a group with colleagues, try not to be the one who always reaches the door first. Although it can sometimes mean politeness, always stepping ahead of the group to open the door sends a subtle message that you think you are in charge.

Be careful with your language at work. Be mindful of the company's hierarchy when addressing people and *never* use foul language. Canadians tend to be more formal with their superiors and more relaxed with colleagues and immediate supervisors. Observe the language used in the office, and try to adapt to it a little more.

Be mindful of how you give feedback. Try to avoid using "but" and respond rather than react to what people say. Before you answer, think of how the other person is going to be affected by what you are about to say. When people react, they say the first thing that comes to their mind regardless if the other person is ready for it or not. By offering a considered response, you show empathy for others.

Try to think of more ways you can compliment instead of criticize others. Turn negative situations into positive ones. If someone has an idea that you don't necessarily agree with, try to find something positive to say about their ideas first before you respond.

Be aware that people may act defensively around you because they've heard about your reputation. In such cases, just try hard to be agreeable and not show any kind of frustration. Let these people see that you are a humble, reasonable, and down-to-earth person.

You don't have to tell everyone that you are trying to change. Be modest. Your colleagues will notice the changes, and share the news with your supervisor! Don't lose heart; keep in mind that it takes a while for people to trust in your changes, so give them time to warm up to the new you.

Conclusion

Working in Canada, like any other place, presents opportunities and challenges. As you can see, the hardest part of the whole process is looking inward and being honest with yourself. The rules are simple, and if you do your best to follow them, you will have much healthier workplace relationships. It takes courage to change your behaviour and image when you are so used to being another way.

Change is difficult because you have been heavily influenced by your upbringing and the culture you were raised in. Many factors contribute to the growth and development of an individual, just as many contribute to the growth and development of any given culture. Since it is impossible to change a culture, we have only one choice: we must change ourselves.

For some people, it may be easy, while for others, it can be hard. Some may need to make just a few minor adjustments to their own behaviour, while others must undergo a major shift. Nevertheless, the results are the same for everyone. Your family and friends will start to see those changes, and they will give you the positive feedback and encouragement you need to continue.

Now I leave you with one last question, as I do in all my communication sessions: *If you could take two or three main points from this book and apply them to your life, what would they be?*

About the Author

Matt Adolphe is an instructor at the Southern Alberta Institute of Technology. He holds a B.A. in Indigenous Studies and History from Laurentian University and an M.A. in Communication Management from the University of South Australia.

Matt's deep Canadian roots date back to the earliest French explorers. His Métis heritage stretches back to the Red River and the North-West Rebellion of the nineteenth century. He was a founding member of the Métis Nation of Ontario and served as its first post-secondary representative.

For over 15 years, he lived and worked in Korea, Japan and Macao. While teaching in Asia, Matt also worked with various media firms ultimately gaining recognition as the first English-language television news presenter in Macao's broadcasting history.

Now back in Canada, Matt designs and teaches courses focused on strengthening workplace communication in the energy and education sectors. Matt lives with his young family in Calgary, Alberta.